COUNT____
—— IN THE ——
RUGBY AREA

Jim Watson

THISWAY
BOOKS

RUGBY • WARWICKSHIRE

ISBN 0-9542999-0-6
First published 2003

THISWAY
BOOKS

Thisway Books, 25 Frobisher Road, Rugby, Warwickshire CV22 7HU
Tel/fax: 01788 813609. e-mail: jim@cartoon.fsbusiness.co.uk

PLEASE NOTE

All these walks are on public rights of way. Most are well-established and it's usually obvious where you can walk. There may, however, be occasional short sections where waymarking has disappeared, fences have been moved, or crops have been planted across the path. Don't panic. Use your common sense. This is the rural Midlands. You can't get lost. Can you?

The sketchmaps are schematic and intended only as guides. Ordnance Survey Explorer maps sheets 221, 222 and 223 cover all of the walks and are highly recommended.

All the walks cross farmland so you will certainly come across farm animals. Assume all of them to be dangerous, even though it's highly unlikely that any of them are – as long as they are left alone. If animals approach you they are probably only being nosy. However, if you have a dog with you they will see it as a threat and may become aggressive to protect their young. Don't run away. They'll think it's a game and will join in like big, boisterous children.

Remember, if anything scary blocks your path you are within your rights to find another route round the obstruction.

Serious incidents, paths blocked or in poor condition should be reported to the appropriate county council: Warwickshire Tel: 00845 090 7000, Northamptonshire Tel: 01604 236 236, or Leicestershire Tel: 0116 265 7086. The author would also welcome news of any changes.
Good walking!

Contents   Page

Symbols used on the maps

 Walking route   Gate   Stile    Foot bridge   Kissing gate

 Parking   Church with spire   Church with tower   Bridge   Buildings

To save space 'right' and 'left' are abbreviated to 'R' and 'L' and 'right hand side' and left hand side' to 'RHS' and 'LHS'.

Northampton Lane

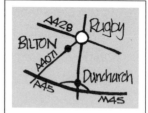

Start & finish Bilton, on the A7071 two miles south-west of Rugby town centre
Terrain Field paths and lanes. No steep hills. Some mud after rain
Time Allow two hours
Parking Free public car parks off Bilton main street
Facilities Shops and two pubs – The George and The Black Horse – at Bilton
Public Transport Bus routes 4 or 5 from Rugby town centre
Map Explorer sheet 222

Bilton has now been enveloped into the sprawl of Rugby but still retains much of its village character. The walk begins along a splendid avenue of lime trees, crosses pleasant pastureland to an ancient highway and returns through a mature housing estate. This is an easy stroll to work up an appetite, walk the dog or wind down in the evening.

1 Begin at the east end of Bilton village. Turn off the main Rugby road into Ashlawn Road, then immediately turn R into Limetree Avenue.

At the end of a remarkable avenue of tall lime trees look for a stile at the LHS of a locked ornamental gateway. Go into a field and follow the boundary of Cawston House to a green lane which climbs gently to Cawston Lane.

Cawston House was the home of Lord John Scott whose statue stands in Dunchurch. His wife, Alice Ann Spottiswoode, wrote the Scottish air *Annie Laurie*

and may also have written *The Bonnie Banks of Loch Lomond.*

Turn L along Cawston Lane for about 100 yards, then climb a stile R into a field. Keep to the wire fence on your R to a wood ahead.

Follow the woodland path through a narrow coppice. Cross the field at

Old Granny's Meat Pies shop

the end, keeping to the hedge on your R. In the next field, cross diagonally to a double-stiled bridge then turn L and follow a hedge to a green lane.

2 This is Northampton Lane, once the main road to Northampton. Although now deeply rutted by modern farm vehicles, and usually muddy after rain, it remains a vital part of living history.

Turn L along the lane then L again at the end to join a surfaced stretch. This swings R, past Windmill Houses but continues as a green (or brown after rain!)

4

lane until Cawston Lane.

Our route turns L off the lane into a field just beyond a farm entrance. Follow the hedge on your L for a short while, then turn R and cross the centre of the field to a line of trees.

Continue through two fields, keeping to the hedge on your L. Cross Cawston Lane onto a bridleway to Dunkleys Farm where the route narrows to an enclosed pathway to Ashlawn Road.

3 Turn L along the road of mature semis and keep walking to a recreation ground. Cross the road to a tarmac road alongside a rugby pitch which takes you through garden allotments into an enclosed pathway. Cross Magnet Lane into another enclosed pathway which ends at Bilton Green.

Old Granny's Meat Pies shop on your L is the oldest building in Bilton.

The village stocks, last used in 1866, are nearby. The George across the road used to be a coaching inn with a smithy behind. St Marks Church, built of red sandstone in 1350 and renowned for its 'grand but quiet beauty', stands on the town side of the village and is well-worth visiting.

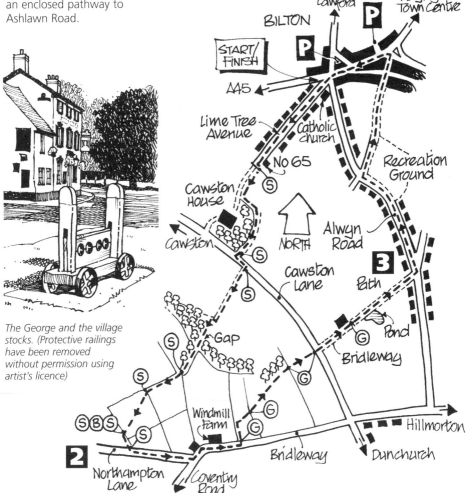

The George and the village stocks. (Protective railings have been removed without permission using artist's licence)

The Oxford Canal

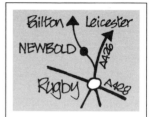

Start & Finish Newbold-on-Avon, on the B4112 Pailton road, one and a half miles from Rugby town centre
Parking With consideration outside Newbold church or at the village shops
Terrain Fields paths, quiet minor roads and canal towpath. No steep hills
Time Allow two hours
Facilities Newbold has shops and three pubs
Public Transport Bus routes 6, 7 and 585 from Rugby town centre
Map Explorer sheet 222

An interesting walk which begins at an ancient church, crosses open countryside, takes in attractive and historic stretches of canal and ends dramatically with a spooky walk through a tunnel.

1 Begin on the path through the churchyard of the 15th century Church of St Botolph. Bear R past the church. Have a look over the hedge at the bricked-up entrance to a 125 yard-long canal tunnel which emerged roughly where the modern road now passes the Boat Inn.

Go over a stile into an avenue of oak trees to a footbridge over a disused canal loop. Bear R through rougher ground to join a tarmac road. Turn L under a railway bridge then immediately turn R through a kissing gate into an open field. 'Admire' a striking view of Rugby Cement Works, then hurry on to cross the fledgling River Avon and climb a hill to an enclosed pathway into an housing estate on the edge of Long Lawford.

Cross a small green to an enclosed path between numbers 45 and 47 Ashman Avenue. Rural views now beckon ahead.

Head diagonally over a large field to the lane which leads to Holbrook Grange, just visible on your R. St John's church on your L is part of the Grange estate.

2 Cross the lane and the next field to a metal gate into a green lane. Extensive views now open up as you climb a hill then descend to some ancient fishing pools and Little Lawford Mill.

Little Lawford Mill

6

Continue round the mill, pause for a look at the ford in the River Avon, then go up the lane past Little Lawford Hall to join the Newbold to King's Newnham minor road. Turn L for a short distance then turn R into another minor road signed 'Harborough Magna 1½ miles'. The road is normally quiet but has broad grass verges to walk on if necessary.

3 Pause at the railway bridge for distant views of both Coventry and Rugby. It's unusual to see both places from the same ground level viewpoint.

The road descends gently to an unclassified country road on your R. This is Cathiron Lane, an ancient byway from Brinklow. The lane can be muddy after rain but in dry conditions it's a wonderfully off-the-beaten-track route to the canal. Avoid the pool and buildings you come to (they are protected by loose dogs and geese). Instead bear R into a narrow green pathway (which may look overgrown, but usually isn't) to a canal bridge.

Go down to the towpath and turn R towards Rugby. After about 300 yards go over an ornamental bridge which crosses the end of the old canal loop from the tunnel at Newbold church.

4 Another 500 yards brings you to Newbold Tunnel, which was built in the 1820s when the canal was straightened. Although the 200 yards-long tunnel is perfectly safe to walk through, the effect of not been able to see where you are putting your feet can be unsettling. If you are of a nervous disposition consider taking a torch. TAKE GREAT CARE WITH CHILDREN. Though they'll probably love the dark, echoing atmosphere. Anxious parents, however, may welcome a stiff drink at either (or both!) of the two pubs situated only 200 yards from the tunnel exit.

A short walk up the village road brings you back to St Botolph's Church.

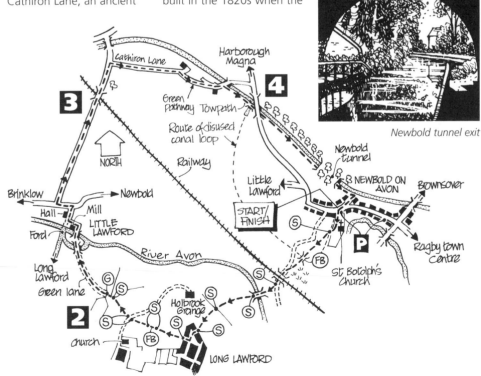

Newbold tunnel exit

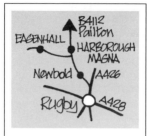

Easenhall village green

Easenhall has one of the prettiest village greens in the area, while the red-brick farm buildings and rural views around Harborough Magna are a surprisingly tranquil contrast to the busy roads nearby. Linked with a historic stretch of the Oxford canal, this is an easy walk of variety and interest for all of the family.

Start & Finish Easenhall, off the B4112 Pailton road, four miles north of Rugby.
Parking Rear car park of the Golden Lion by kind permission of the landlord, Jim Austin
Terrain Field paths, canal towpath and quiet minor roads. No steep hills. Muddy patches after rain
Time Allow two hours
Facilities Two pubs, The Golden Lion at Easenhall and The Old Lion at Harborough Magna
Public Transport Bus route 585 to Harborough Magna from Rugby town centre
Map Explorer sheet 222

1 Begin at Easenhall green. Go down a narrow walled path beside the village hall and cross two fields to the railway. Cross a footbridge and another field to the Oxford canal. Go over a canal bridge and turn L down to the towpath. Turn R and walk towards Rugby.

2 After passing under two canal bridges you arrive at the hamlet of Cathiron, once the site of Iven's timber yard. Teams of horses and men from Harborough Magna used to haul huge trees felled on the Lawford estate to

Rugby station for sawing up and transportation. Canal barges carried seasoned timber direct from here to the factories.

Leave the towpath at the first canal bridge you come to after going under the railway. Turn L along a broad lane, once a busy coach and horses route, which takes you to the Easenhall road. Turn L along it and then first R into the quiet minor road signed 'Harborough Magna village only'.

At the edge of the village turn L up Back Lane for some good views of the

church and mellow red farm buildings. The end of the lane returns you to a noisier modern age on the Newbold to Pailton road, within sight – and sound – of the M6 motorway. Turn R and walk along the roadside into the village passing the wooden village hall and a terrace of old cottages.

3 The nearby Old Lion Inn had to be fully restored after a disastrous fire in 1986. Turn R up the

Harborough Magna

road opposite the Old Lion, passing mature farm buildings, the Georgian Home Farm and the Old Rectory. The ancient clock-face on the 14th century tower of All Saint's Church was restored in 1983, when a new design showing the four Evangelists was added.

Continue down Main Street, away from the church and pass the nursery school, built in 1845. At the edge of the village, climb a style on your R and cross three fields back to Easenhall.

The small village is well-worth exploring. A huge 'listed' barn with a high archway dominates the pretty village green, while in glorious contrast nearby stands a tiny fairy-tale cottage. Villagers bought the single-roomed, former congregational chapel for use as a hall. The Golden Lion has been much-improved over the years, but still has some original waffle and daub walls which date back to 1640.

Some wonderful Gothic semis next door were built for workers on the nearby Newbold Revel estate. An attractive half-timbered cottage on the far outskirts of the village has straw peacocks woven into its thatched roof.

The Oxford canal at Cathiron

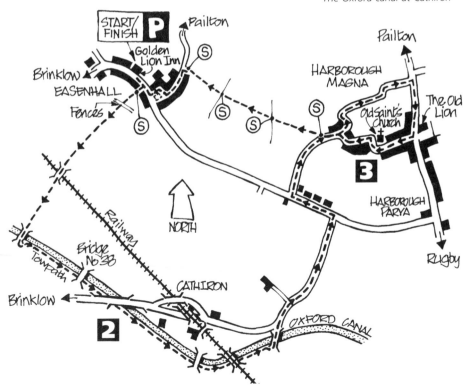

9

4. Swift Valley & Oxford Canal   4 miles/6.4km

Swift aqueduct

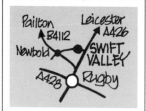

Start/finish Swift Valley country park off the A426 near Brownsover, two miles north of Rugby town centre
Parking Public car park
Terrain Field paths, lanes, bridleway and canal towpath. Some gentle climbing and muddy patches after rain.
Time Allow two hours
Facilities The Harvester, near Brownsover
Public Transport None suitable
Map Explorer sheet 222

Starting at a council-owned country park, this walk takes in two sections of canal heritage, climbs to some good rural views and returns along a peaceful corridor through a modern industrial estate.

1 From the country park car park go through a metal gate on an obvious path. This soon swings L alongside a disused canal, now a feeder from the River Swift, north of the M6 motorway.

Cross a red-brick bridge over the canal and turn L to follow the other bank. In sight of the M6 motorway, turn L over a concrete footbridge, then bear R to a bench, one of a series along the route designed by local school children.

2 Continue along a track through light woodland, which covers another old loop of the canal, abandoned in the 1830s when the main canal was straightened. Pause at the remains of the Cosford Aqueduct which once carried the canal over the River Swift. Steep wooden steps descend to the riverside from where you can admire the massive brickwork, dating back to when the canal was first built in the 1700s.

Turn R after the aqueduct and follow the edge of a field uphill. Go L along Cosford Lane towards modern factory buildings. After about 200 yards, turn

The bridge over the canal arm

R onto an 'unclassified' country road heading back towards Cosford.

Swing L at some farm buildings and climb steadily over a disused railway, once the Rugby to Leicester line. The view now becomes more open with Rugby visible on your L. Go past a shooting area at the top of the hill where there's ample evidence of clay pigeons – shattered and unbroken (missed!). Obviously, take care if shooting is going on.

3 When the metalled lane ends, bear left to join a bridleway along the edge of a field. Follow a hedge on your R to the top side of the field, then turn L onto a track heading towards Rugby.

Cross two fields on an obvious route, rising to a broad hilltop from where the village of Newbold and the Oxford canal can be see on your R.

Continue to the Brownsover Road. As it is often busy with fast traffic, stay in the field and turn L to walk just inside the hedge parallel to the road. At the corner of the field, cross the road (look out for fast traffic!) to a lorry turning area.

Go through a gate onto a grassy track, once another part of the Rugby to Leicester line. This soon shrinks to a path through bushes to canal bridge No52 on the edge of The Glebe housing estate.

4 Go down steps and turn R along the canal towpath. Cross an attractive iron bridge over the Willow Wren arm of the canal and continue

along an aqueduct section over the old Leicester Road.

Keep walking to The Harvester public house. Cross a footbridge over the canal, pausing to admire a tall bullrushes sculpture, then turn L along the bank of the canal feeder arm.

Curve R under a modern concrete bridge and continue to a more attractive red-brick bridge. Leave the path to cross the old Leicester Road, then return to the waterside amongst tall trees around Brownsover Hall Hotel. The car park is across the country park to your L.

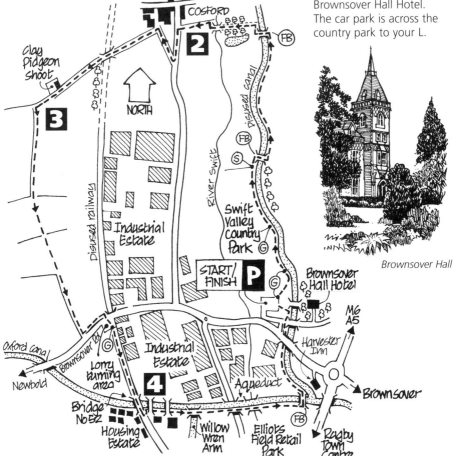

Brownsover Hall

11

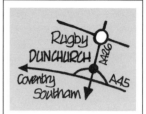

Start & Finish Dunchurch, on the A426, three miles south of Rugby town centre
Parking Dunchurch Square or with consideration on the streets
Terrain Field paths, pavement and bridleway. Some gentle climbing
Time Allow two hours
Facilities Shops and pubs in Dunchurch village
Public Transport Bus route 5 from Rugby town centre.
Map Explorer sheet 222

St Peter's Church, Dunchurch

An easy-going family walk through the hidden pathways of the attractive and historic village of Dunchurch, and the surrounding countryside.

1 Begin at St Peter's Church. Walk through the churchyard and along an enclosed pathway to a road. Turn R and cross a drive which goes to Dunchurch Conference Centre. Enter an enclosed pathway running parallel with a private road alongside Bilton Grange School. Continue through a sports field and a meadow. Cross Bilton Grange drive and enter yet another enclosed pathway.

Emerging at the Dunchurch to Rugby road, turn R along the pavement and keep on it to a roundabout. Cross to a walkway along the LHS of Ashlawn Road (the RHS of the road is a cycleway).

2 As it straightens after an 's' bend, cross the road (with care!) and go through a gap in a hedge signed 'bridleway'. Keep straight on, following the hedge on your L, to an

Track over the Rainsbrook

obvious route down a grassy hill. The bleak aspect of the Onley prisons, built on the site of an old army camp, rather taints the rural view ahead. However, with Barby Hill to the L and the broad Vale of Evesham stretching into the distance, it's still a scene to enjoy.

At the bottom of the hill, turn R through a gap in a wire fence. Follow the Rainsbrook, a stream which marks the Warwickshire and Northamptonshire border, to a track.

Turn L onto the track and cross the Rainsbrook, then immediately turn R through a gap in the hedge into a field. Follow the brook L to the M45. At the embankment, cross the footbridge on your R and keep to the fence alongside the motorway to a noisy rookery. Bear R, following the edge of the field to an open area at the junction of three fields. Take the green track along the LHS of the middle field.

Prominent on the hilltop ahead are Bilton Grange School and Dunchurch Lodge (now a conference centre), once very grand private houses.

3 Just before a clump of trees, turn L through a gap in a hedge. Keep to another hedge on your R and go over a stile into a pasture. Follow the hedge on your L up a hill.

Halfway up the pasture, find a double stile and a footbridge in the hedge. Cross into the bottom

corner of the next field then head diagonally towards the house in the top L corner.

Go through a gate and follow a hedge L to a stile onto the Dunchurch to Braunston road. Turn R along the pavement and climb the hill back into the village.

Situated at the crossing of the Oxford to Leicester and Coventry to Northampton roads, Dunchurch was a important stopping place in the mail coach days. Up to 40 coaches a day would stop to change horses.

Of the many coaching

Guy Fawkes House

inns only The Dun Cow and The Green Man remain. Guy Fawkes House was possibly the Lion Inn, where the 1605 Gunpowder Plot conspirators waited in vain to hear if their plan had succeeded.

A church has stood in Dunchurch for over 1000 years. Most of St Peter's is 14th century with the tower added in the 15th.

13

Braunston

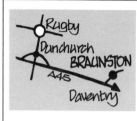

Start/finish Braunston, on the A45 seven miles south of Rugby town centre
Parking The Millhouse public house on the A45. (You are going to be a patron when you return, aren't you?)
Terrain Field paths and bridleway. Some gentle climbing and mud after rain
Time Allow three hours
Facilities The Millhouse. Two more pubs and shops in Braunston village
Public Transport Bus route GA2 from Church St, Rugby
Map Explorer sheet 222

Braunston is a large, handsome village set on a ridge overlooking a large marina and the junction of the Grand Union and Oxford canals. This walk also explores the area's rich railway heritage, and passes the sites of two ancient 'lost' villages.

1 From the car park cross a road bridge and turn R onto the canal towpath. Go over a beautiful iron bridge at the junction of the Oxford and Grand Union canals and pass boat moorings to a road bridge. Climb steps to the roadside and go over a way-marked stile in the hedge on your L.

Head diagonally across the field to a gate which opens onto a bridleway. This follows a line of trees straight to a bridge in the railway embankment which once carried the Great Central line between Rugby and Woodford Halse.

2 Pause to admire the monumental design and brickwork of the bridge before following the hedge on your R across four fields, climbing gradually to the impressive Willoughby House. Keep R of the

house, following a line of chestnut trees parallel to the drive to a small gate onto a minor road. A public right of way soon leaves the road to go L across fields between two farms, both confusingly called 'Leam Farm'.

Sawbridge is an oddly scattered hamlet of broad grass verges and ancient farms. Continue past the second Leam Farm to the centre of a field, then turn L onto a well-defined bridleway.

Junction of the Grand Union and Oxford canals

3 The views from here across Warwickshire and Northamptonshire are extensive. The River Leam, meandering through the fields on your L, forms the country boundary.

After about a mile of level walking, the bridleway rises to cross a high bridge over the Grand Union canal and another crossing the dismantled Central Railway. The Braunston to Long Itchington line also once came through here, running parallel with our route. The two lines actually crossed just a field away on your R.

Continue past the Hall to the 13th century church of St Peter's, all that remains – apart from the grassy mounds opposite the church – of Wolfhampcote. The village probably died in the 18th century when its inhabitants were turned out during the land enclosures. Parts of St Peter's date back to the 13th century. The small, lonely church is now rarely used for worship but remains well-cared for, a potent reminder, with the closed-down railway lines, of how country life can change dramatically. Indeed, further on just past the church is the site of another 'lost' village, Braunstonebury.

4 The modern village of Braunston can now be seen ahead, with the tall spire of All Saint's church, an old windmill, (blessedly finding a new role as a dwelling house) and the white-painted rectory making a glorious picture to end the walk.

Continue on the bridleway to the road bridge over the canal and sustenance at the Millhouse, itself a restoration of an old canal-side pub. The regeneration of the canal system has been a remarkably Good Thing, bringing new life (and walkways) to the countryside. In times of great change, not all of it is necessary for the worse.

An additional stroll along the towpath to the marina and back through Braunston village is highly recommended.

St Peter's Church, Wolfhampcote

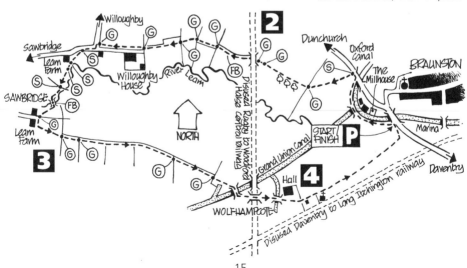

15

Churchover Green

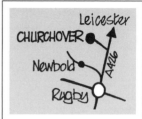

Start/finish Churchover village, off the A426 four miles north of Rugby town centre
Parking With consideration on the village streets. Outside the church is okay. (Not on Sundays though!)
Terrain Field paths, lanes, and bridleways. Some climbing and mud after rain.
Time Allow three hours
Facilities Churchover village pub, The Haywagon.
Public Transport Sparse service. Bus route X40 from Clifton road, Rugby
Maps Explorer sheet 222

Based at the peaceful village of Churchover, this route crosses farmland straddling the M6 motorway. It's relatively short but surprisingly satisfying. There's extensive views from a hilltop between Churchover and Harborough Magna.

1 Begin walking at the cross roads near the Haywagon public house, where a flamboyantly twisted tree shades a small village green.

Go over a stile L of the last house below the pub and walk down the hill in the meadow to the meandering River Swift. Cross a footbridge near a sluicegate and go behind a small environmental agency building to cross another waterway using a double stile and a footbridge.

Turn L to face Harborough Fields Farm on the hill near an archway in the railway embankment. Cross a field to a stile in the corner beside the stumps of four willow trees.

Keep straight on across the next field. Go through an iron gate and cross the next field to a waymarking pole in the top LH corner. Climb the steep disused railway embankment and go down the other side.

Keep to the hedge on your L across two fields. Where the hedge begins to curve R, find a two stiles and footbridge combination

Cosford

on your L. Cross into a meadow and head just R of an electric pylon to a waymarked stile in the hedge ahead.

2 Climb the hill in the next meadow bearing R to a water trough.

Continue climbing, heading for a waymarking pole in the field just L of the houses on the skyline.

Cross two stiles and a narrow field onto the Harborough Magna road. Turn L and walk along the roadside past St Mary's Nursing

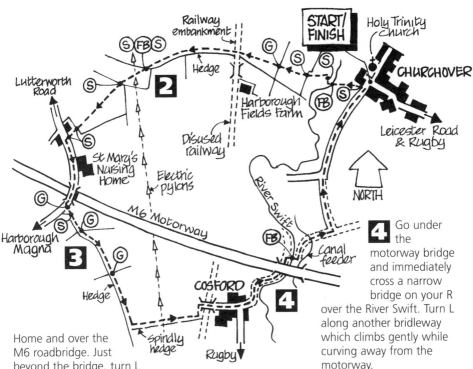

Home and over the M6 roadbridge. Just beyond the bridge, turn L through a gate into an enclosed area with a lane leading off. Ignore the lane. Instead, go over a stile ahead and join a bridleway which keeps to the hedge on your R.

3 Continue through three fields, climbing steadily to a hilltop from where there's extensive views to Rugby, Churchover and Harborough Magna. At a spindly hedge, turn L to face downhill with the M6 Rugby turn-off ahead.

Continue down the hillside and cross an old bridge over another part of the disused Rugby to Leicester railway. Join a lane which takes you through the hamlet of Cosford. Keep straight on past the road junction to Swift Valley industrial estate and take a rough, meandering lane to the embankment of the M6 motorway.

The bridleway turn-off to Churchover

4 Go under the motorway bridge and immediately cross a narrow bridge on your R over the River Swift. Turn L along another bridleway which climbs gently while curving away from the motorway.

About 200 yards beyond a canal feeder stream, turn L onto another bridleway. This climbs steeply before joining the minor road back to Churchover.

You will pass a North Sea Gas distribution installation which was controversially built just outside the village during the early 1970s.

Churchover is an attractive mixture of the old and the new. Holy Trinity church, which was restored in the late 19th century, stands proudly on a hilltop, its 15th century tower and spire a much admired landmark from miles around.

17

The River Leam at Marton

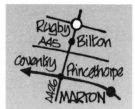

Start/finish Marton, on the A423 eight miles south-west of Rugby town centre
Parking Recycling area next to The Black Horse public house or at the recreation ground, Luisa Ward Close.
Terrain Field paths, lanes and quiet minor roads. Some gentle climbing
Time Allow two and a half hours
Facilities Pubs at Marton and Frankton
Public Transport None suitable
Map Explorer sheets 221 and 222

An excellent family walk between two attractive villages which goes through surprisingly hilly country giving good views across the Warwickshire and Northamptonshire countryside. With a pub at each end, it's a perfect route for a warm summer's evening.

1 Begin on the Middleton Bridge over the River Leam. Built of honey-coloured stone in 1414, it was replaced in 2001 by a modern concrete bridge alongside.

Go through a gate in a hedge on the north side of the bridge and cross a field to the riverside. Continue on an obvious path through three more fields to the B4455 Fosse Way.

Turn R along the grass verge, then R again into a minor road (unsigned) which climbs steadily, giving good views across Marton to Leamington Spa before descending to the A423 Coventry to Southam road. Cross with care to a footpath on the other side.

2 Turn R and walk back towards Marton for about 150 yards, then turn L up an unfenced lane towards Windmill Hill. The lane curves R around the base of the hill (the windmill is long gone) towards a distant house.

The Friendly Inn at Frankton

Our route continues straight ahead through a wide iron gate and across the side of the field at the base of the hill.

Go through another iron gate to join a bridleway which climbs to an excellent viewpoint giving good all round views to the Vale of Evesham and Princethorpe College.

Keep on the bridleway as it joins a pleasant back road into the sleepy village of Frankton. Take

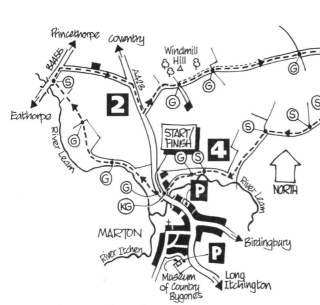

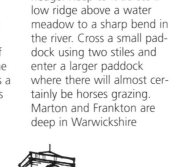

a horseshoe route through the village. Pass neat modern house and perhaps pause awhile at the half-timbered Friendly Inn.

3 Continue down the lane past the inn through the older part of the village. The handsome church of St Nicholas has a 13th century tower but is mostly Victorian restoration. The Manor House next to it dates back to 1662 and has its own fish pools which you pass further down the lane.

Beyond the second pool, where the lane swings L, go over a stile straight ahead into a field. Follow the hedge on your L along the sides of two pastures. When almost across a third pasture – long and narrow –

and with the river in sight ahead, bear R up a hill to a hedge. Keep to it across a low ridge above a water meadow to a sharp bend in the river. Cross a small paddock using two stiles and enter a larger paddock where there will almost certainly be horses grazing. Marton and Frankton are deep in Warwickshire

St Esprit's Church, Marton

horsey country. Horses are big and slightly worrying to non-horsey people but generally they only want to check you out and be friendly. However, please do NOT feed them.

4 Follow the hedge on your R and pass The Elms, a lovely half-timbered farmhouse which could have come straight out of Radio 4's 'The Archers'. Continue through a kissing gate back onto the bridge over the Leam.

Marton suffers traffic pollution from the busy A423 but away from the main road it's a tranquil and attractive village. The delightful parish church of St Esprit dates back to the 12th century but had to be largely rebuilt in 1871 after a disastrous fire. Further along the lane, The Old Brew House, now a picturesque private dwelling, hints at an earlier industrial use. Luisa Ward Close leads to the Museum of Country Bygones, run by local historian, George Tims.

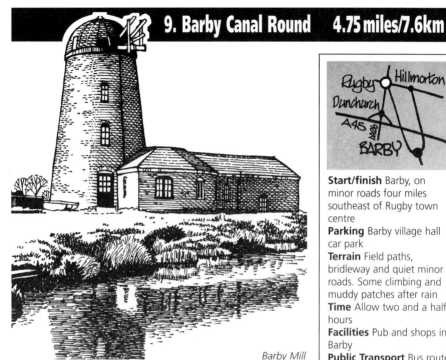

Barby Mill

Start/finish Barby, on minor roads four miles southeast of Rugby town centre
Parking Barby village hall car park
Terrain Field paths, bridleway and quiet minor roads. Some climbing and muddy patches after rain
Time Allow two and a half hours
Facilities Pub and shops in Barby
Public Transport Bus route 88/89 from Rugby town centre. Meagre service
Map Explorer sheet 222

A bright and breezy circuit across farmland and along ancient byways, taking in the area's highest point Barby Hill. Superb panoramic views.

1 Begin at the village hall car park. Turn R along Kilsby Road to the main road, then turn L up a hill to a sign 'Footpath to Ashby St Ledgers'. Turn L as indicated between the bungalows numbered 33 and 35 onto an enclosed path.

Cross a series of waymarked paddocks heading diagonally across a hillside to a minor road, The Ridgeway. As you climb, an extensive view opens up to your L with the freight depot at Crick and the airshafts of the Kilsby rail tunnel prominent.

2 Turn R along The Ridgeway to a crossroads. Cross the main road and go down a lane signed 'Footpath' to the L of a water tower and a radio mast. Pass Barby Mill, where a renovated windmill makes an attractive picture

The track to the Rugby road

across a fishery pool.

The obvious route continues straight ahead across variable terrain; tarmac, gravel, grass and extremely rough – and muddy after rain – bridleway. As you will have seen earlier on this walk, horses are a big part of village life here and this part of our route is one of their favourite exercise routes. However, the extensive views make up for any inconvenience underfoot.

Pause where a track joins R from some farm buildings. This is approximately the summit

20

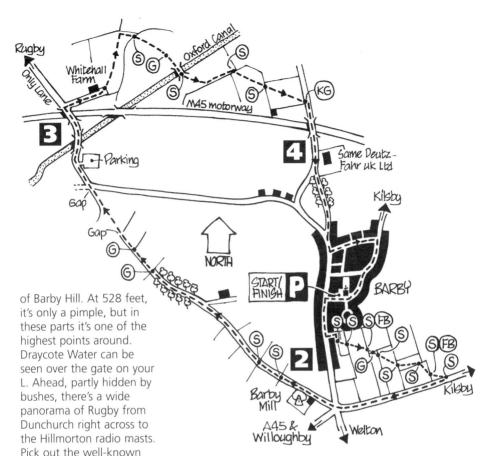

of Barby Hill. At 528 feet, it's only a pimple, but in these parts it's one of the highest points around. Draycote Water can be seen over the gate on your L. Ahead, partly hidden by bushes, there's a wide panorama of Rugby from Dunchurch right across to the Hillmorton radio masts. Pick out the well-known landmarks then continue downhill along a worn track across farmland to the Barby to Rugby road.

3 Keep straight on, over the canal and the M45, then turn R down a concrete lane to Whitehall Farm. Enjoy the old railway signs displayed in humorous positions around the farmyard. Go into a field through the gate with a sign which threatens you with a fine of 'forty shillings' (£2) if you leave it open. Cross to the far end of the field where

there's a fine view of Hillmorton ahead, then turn sharp R and follow a hedge to a stile. Cross two fields to a bridge over the canal. Bear L across the next field, then follow a hedge L to a stile in the corner.

Head diagonally over the next two fields to join a minor road, Barby Lane. Turn R along the road and cross the M45. Just past the Same Deutz-Fahr UK Ltd industrial unit, turn L up a rather overgrown (and probably muddy) bridleway which climbs back to Barby.

Old buildings clustered around the church are the most attractive part of the village. The tower of the ancient parish Church of St Mary is a familiar landmark from miles around.

Barby

21

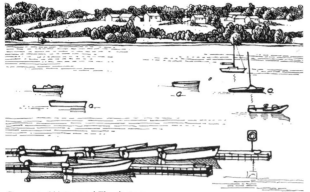

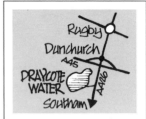

Draycote Water and Thurlaston

Location On the A426 Southam road, 4 miles southwest of Rugby town centre
Terrain Flat road around Draycote Water. Another road in the Country Park climbs to Hensborough Hill
Time Allow two and a half hours
Parking Pay and display in the Country Park
Facilities Fishing lodge
Public Transport Bus route 63 from Clifton Road, Rugby

Draycote Water would probably not be the first choice route for the 'purist' country walker. However, with good views, abundant birdlife and an open aspect, the reservoir and Country Park are a considerable attraction. Access (every day except Christmas day) is free for walkers, joggers, cyclists and wheelchair users. Motorists must obtain a permit to use the road.

The route is simple – you just walk round the reservoir on the road.

There are three access points: from the Country Park, on foot from Thurlaston, or crossing a field from Toft on the outskirts of Dunchurch.

I like to walk anti-clockwise so the fine view across the water to Thurlaston village is in front of me.

1 During the fishing season (April to October), begin walking on the road alongside the Farnborough Dam to avoid the long lines being cast by anglers along the top. Keep well clear of angler's back-casts all round the reservoir.

In the close season (November to March) it's safe to walk along the top, from where there's an extensive view across open countryside to Barby and the industrial units at Crick.

A fine bird hide has been built at the end of the dam overlooking Toft Bay. Draycote Water is a haven for a vast range of wildfowl and birdlife. Recent sightings are displayed on a board situated in the road to the fishing lodge.

2 Through light woodland, the road turns sharp L passing the access gate from Toft. This part of the route is the most natural, with the road winding around small inlets and wildfowl roosting across the lakeshore – and even on the golf course!

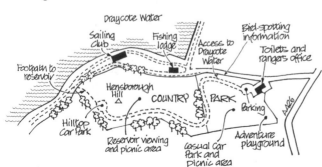

22

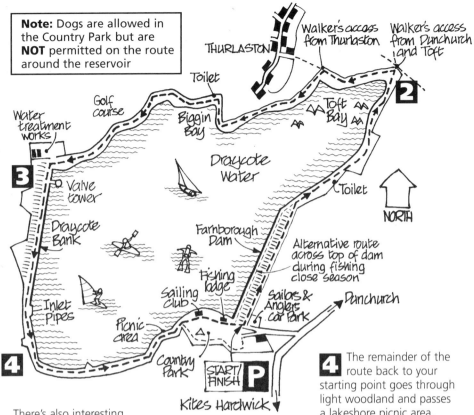

Note: Dogs are allowed in the Country Park but are **NOT** permitted on the route around the reservoir

THURLASTON

Walker's access from Thurlaston

Walker's access from Dunchurch and Toft

Toilet

Golf course

Biggin Bay

Toft Bay

2

Water treatment works

3

Valve tower

Draycote Water

Toilet

NORTH

Draycote Bank

Farnborough Dam

Alternative route across top of dam during fishing close season

Fishing lodge

Inlet pipes

Sailing Club

Sailors & Anglers car park

Dunchurch

Picnic area

4

Country Park

START/FINISH **P**

Kites Hardwick

There's also interesting views of the fine houses and farms which overlook the lake.

3 The final section of the circuit takes you onto another dam, Draycote Bank. As before, use the road if anglers are casting along the dam top.

Prominent in the water is the Valve Tower, which is part of the Severn Trent water treatment works. From inside the tower, engineers can assess the clarity of water below the surface and decide at which level extraction should take place.

From the Draycote Bank there's good views to

Draycote village and across countryside to Leamington Spa. The ponds below the dam were once used to breed fish for the reservoir. Now delivered by tanker from the south of England, stocks are replenished twice a week during the season.

In 2002, 50,000 rainbow trout, ranging from 1.5lbs to over 10lbs in weight, were introduced. Each angler can take up to eight fish on a day permit.

At the end of the dam you can see water flowing into Draycote Water from Stamford reservoir and a collection point on the River Leam at Eathorpe.

4 The remainder of the route back to your starting point goes through light woodland and passes a lakeshore picnic area.

An exploration of the Country Park, owned by Warwickshire County Council, is a good way to end the walk. Hensborough Hill is an excellent viewpoint and a good place for a picnic.

The Valve Tower

Coombe Abbey

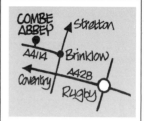

Start/finish Coombe Country Park, off the B4027 eight miles west of Rugby town centre
Parking Country Park pay car park. The £2 fee may seem excessive but consider it your entrance fee. When you have seen the beautiful grounds you will think the cost worth-while
Terrain Bridleway and lanes. Expect muddy patches after rain
Time Allow 3 hours
Facilities Cafe and tourist shop at Coombe Park
Public Transport Bus routes 570/580 from Rugby town centre
Map Explorer sheet 222

An easy walk through the exotic and beautiful grounds of Coombe Park and the ancient woodland between the Park and Binley Woods.

1 Start at the car park and cross the main drive to a visitor centre building. Keep on a descending road to a wildfowl pool and a splendid view of the east wing of Coombe Abbey.

Continue straight ahead on a hard surfaced path following the Centenary Way signs. Go through an arboretum and bear L to pass Top Pool, pausing to admire the wildfowl and swans. Continue past a toilet block and take a path going R, passing some animal sculptures on a tree in a clearing.

Follow the woodland path on a circular route around a large duck decoy pool to rejoin your original path near Top Pool.

Wrautums Field is a large open, grassy area surrounded by trees – a good place for a picnic.

Little Wrautums is a smaller clearing with magnificent rhododendron bushes. Dogs can be exercised under control in these two areas. Elsewhere in the park they must be kept on leads.

From Top Pool take the path to the hotel buildings, passing lawns and giant conifers on your R. Go through a gate and turn L along a road to pass the entrance to The Abbeygate, a popular venue for society weddings. Keep on the

Twelve O'Clock Ride

road as it curves R. Lookout for an ancient wall and the abbey moat on your R.

Keep to the fence on your L through the hotel car park, a barbecue area and the public car park. You can keep on this exit route but will have to climb a locked gate to gain access to the B4027. You may prefer to turn R onto the main drive to the road.

2 Turn L along the B4027 for about 500 yards, then turn R onto a lane signed 'Birchley Wood

Farmhouse'. Take care along the busy B4027. There is a grass verge wide enough to walk on.

Keep on the lane until it swings L to the farm. Our route joins an enclosed bridleway straight ahead, which runs alongside Birchley Wood. The rather narrow way is popular with horse riders so can be a bit rough underfoot in places.

Follow the edge of the wood on gently rising ground to the corner of a field. Find a gate into the wood R, and go through a short stretch of woodland.

Coombe Abbey was founded by Cistercian monks in 1150. By the 13th century it had become the richest monastic house in the county. After dissolution in 1539 it was owned by the Craven family for more than 300 years. Capability Brown landscaped the grounds. Coventry Council now owns the 400 acres parkland. The house has been recently converted to an hotel.

The Abbeygate

3 Emerge into a large field. Turn R and walk around the perimeter towards Merton Hall Farm. Just before the farm buildings, turn R through a gate to cross a narrow field onto a cinder track beyond the farmhouse.

Turn R along the track. As you approach the main Brandon to Coventry road turn R onto the obvious track through the wood which heads straight as an arrow for around one and a half miles back to Coombe Park.

Halfway along, you emerge from the wood onto an ancient track, Twelve O'Clock Ride, where it's easy to imagine fine horse-drawn carriages heading, Jane Austen-like, for the big house at the end.

25

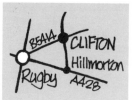

Newton

A splendidly reassuring walk between two old villages, taking-in a beautifully-kept stretch of canal and a disused railway line brought back to life as a popular walkway. With a picnic site halfway round and rural views across the Avon Valley this a route for all the family to enjoy.

Start/finish Clifton upon Dunsmore, on the Clifton Road two miles east of Rugby town centre
Parking Recycling centre car park beside the church
Terrain Field paths, canal towpath, walkways and quiet minor roads. Some gentle climbing
Time Allow three hours
Facilities Pub and shops at Clifton. Pubs also at Newton and St Thomas's Cross
Public Transport Bus route 2 from Rugby town centre
Map Explorer sheet 222

1 Start outside Clifton churchyard. Go up a enclosed pathway across the road from the lych-gate. At the end of the pathway, turn L for a short distance, then cross a road to a pathway between modern houses. Keep on the well-signed path across five open fields with panoramic views of Rugby across a large pond.

Turn R along the Clifton to Hillmorton road. Walk on the broad grass verge down the hill, keeping a lookout for fast traffic. At the first bridge, turn R onto the canal towpath and walk towards Rugby.

2 Pass Rugby golf course, where a disused railway viaduct curves beautifully above the greens. It once carried the Market Harborough to Rugby up line. On the other side of the canal, an embankment still crosses the hill to the long-gone station at Clifton.

Go under the Rugby to Clifton road and pass a

Rugby from near Clifton

boatyard. The remains of another rail crossing (the Market Harborough down line) can be seen just before Butlers Leap Industrial Estate. An elevated section of canal follows, which over-looks playing fields.

At Mill Gardens (which aren't gardens but rather gloomy pools overhung by large trees 30 feet below the level of the canal) go down to poolside and turn R under the aqueduct bridge to the edge of Brownsover housing estate.

St Mary's Church, Clifton

3 You can cross a grassy area on your R to climb a steep embankment onto the Great Central Walk (from where there are fine views across fields to Clifton). But if you prefer not to make the climb, stay on the footpath from the bridge to an estate road. Turn right R along the road, then R again along Stavely Way to join the Walk.

Great Central Walk, kept tidy and trimmed by Rugby Borough Council, is remarkably pleasant with fine views between the trees to Clifton and a couple of fine old railway bridges to admire.

Eventually, you arrive at a railed pathway zig-zagging out of the old cutting up to a picnic site at road level.

Turn R and walk through Newton village, passing the thatched Stag and Pheasant public house and the delightful Good Shepherd Church.

At the edge of the village, take a tarmac footpath along the LHS of the road and go down the hill to the St Thomas's Cross public house. Take care at the cross roads. A footpath beside Newton Road climbs through attractive countryside back to Clifton. A detour around some of the village is recommended, returning past the Bull Inn to the car park.

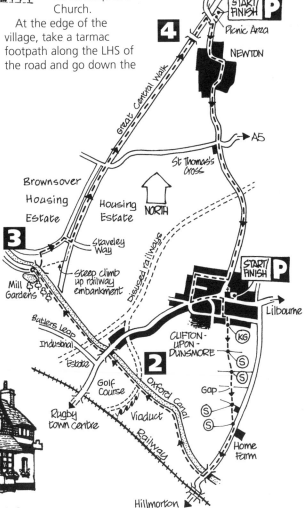

St Thomas's Cross

Approaching Monks Kirby

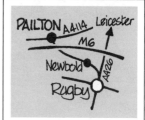

Start/finish Pailton village, off the A426 four miles north of Rugby town centre
Parking Car park at the Ex-Service and Social Club. You're welcome to buy a drink there too!
Terrain Field paths and quiet lanes. Some gentle climbing and mud after rain
Time Allow two and a half hours
Facilities Shop and pub in Pailton. Shop and two pubs in Monks Kirby
Public Transport Bus route 585 from Rugby town centre
Maps Explorer sheet 222

This route around the shallow valley of the Smite Brook connects the villages of Pailton and Monks Kirby. With good views, a magnificent church and even a small lake, this is a walk of quiet surprises.

1 Start at the club car park on the outskirts of Pailton and take a hard surfaced path enclosed by wire fences to Monks Kirby.

Enter the village past the Bell Inn and the Denbigh Arms to the Priory Church of St Edith, the grandest village church in the region. Its mighty sandstone tower has been a landmark for centuries. The Benedictine priory was founded in 1077.

From the church, bear R round a bend in the road and turn R into Brockhurst Road. Pass the post office, Revel School and the war memorial.

2 Where the road swings L at the edge of the village, turn R past Drumgate Cottage into a short lane. This goes into Newnham Paddox Park which, as signs make clear, is strictly private. A grand mansion on the estate was demolished in 1952.

Our route turns R just before the park gate and

Longhouse in Pailton

enters a very large field which usually grows arable crops. The public right of way runs straight across the middle of the field, but depending on the time of year and possibly your stroppiness to assert your rights, you may prefer to pick your way around the field perimeter. Head for a piece of woodland up the hill to your L, charmingly called 'Cabbage Clump'.

At the far end of

28

the field, find a gap in the hedge and, keeping L of a lone tree, cross the next field to a flat bridge over a stream. Do not cross!

Instead, keep straight on and walk along the L bank of the Smite Brook to a metal fence. You are now facing a large (and possibly soggy after rain) field.

Cross diagonally, heading for a clump of conifer trees on the far side. Go through a gap and keep straight on up the hill from where you will see a track curving into a wood. Join the track but do not go into the wood. Instead, keep to the public right of way which skirts the wood.

The White Lion, Pailton

3 From the hilltop at the far corner of the wood, head straight across two large fields aiming for the hamlet of Little Walton. Join a lane and immediately turn R for about 15 yards, then go over a stile on your R into a field. Keep straight on along the edge of the field then turn L onto a path across the hillside.

A splendid walk follows, crossing undulating fields with good views across the valley to Newnham Paddox Park and your outward route from Monks Kirby.

Cross a track lined by a wonderful avenue of oak trees and a further six clearly way-marked fields. This brings you to a lovely pond inhabited by wild-fowl. Known locally as 'The Lake', it's a splendid spot for a summer picnic.

4 Continue on the obvious track back to Pailton. Keep to the hedge on your R and climb to the top end of the village. Turn R down the Lutterworth Road and walk through the village. Pass the post office and the White Lion (good food) back to the club car park.

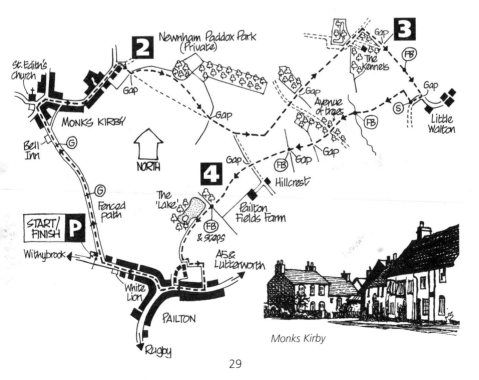

Monks Kirby

Church Hill, Stretton-on-Dunsmore

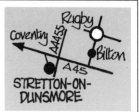

STRETTON-ON-DUNSMORE

Start/finish Stretton-on-Dunsmore, off the A45 four miles west of Rugby town centre
Parking With consideration on the village street.
Terrain Field paths, lanes, bridleway and quiet minor roads. Some gentle climbing and mud after rain
Time Allow three hours
Facilities Two pubs and a shop in Stretton. Pub at Princethorpe
Public Transport Bus routes 570 & 580 from Rugby town centre
Maps Explorer sheets 221 and 222

The rich, open countryside south of Stretton and Princethorpe is always a pleasure to wander. This varied walk also takes in a woodland nature reserve and is probably best enjoyed in early summer sunshine when the bluebells are in glorious bloom.

1 Begin walking down the lane past the Shoulder of Mutton pub. Across the car park a sign welcomes you to 'Coffin Walk ... reinstated by Stretton-on-Dunsmore scouts 1994'.

Cross a series of stiles to a track coming down the hill on your R. Keep straight on, following a wire fence on your R to a stile in the top RH corner of a field. Join a well-established path between a wire fence and a brook.

Go over a track, passing some locked gates on your R, and keep to the hedge on your R across a field. Cross a lane, which goes to Park Farm, and go down a gravel drive to Stretton

Princethorpe College

Fields Cottage. Go past the house and keep R of the garages. Keep to the hedge on your R across a small field, then cross diagonally over the next field to an enclosed pathway into Princethorpe.

Turn L up a minor road, then turn R along the Fosse Way to the Three Horse Shoes public house. Cross the busy A423 road (with care!), go down the hill and turn L along the the B4453 road through Princethorpe.

2 At the last house in the pretty hamlet, turn L through a gap in the

30

hedge onto a grassy track along the edge of a large field, from where there's a fine view of Princethorpe College.

Begun in 1832 as the Priory of St Mary for Benedictine nuns driven from France by the 1792 revolution, the complex of glowing red buildings built of clay bricks dug from the site, is now a private school. The massive tower of the Pugin designed New Church dominates the area.

About half way across the field, go through a gap in the hedge on your L and continue walking in the same direction on the other side. Where the hedge ends on a hilltop, keep straight on down the hill to cross a footbridge and a stile.

Bear R across a small field to two metal gates in the far corner. Go through the gate on the L and keep to the hedge on your R. At the far side of the field, turn sharp R and go straight up the side of a

All Saint's Church

field to Hill Farm. Cross the road (WITH CARE!) and join a track curving R to Wappenbury Wood, a Nature Reserve managed by Warwickshire Wildlife Trust.

3 At 'Shady Acres', a private house on the north side of the wood, turn R along a minor road. At the first junction, turn L

onto another minor road. Pass Burnthurst Farm and, where the road eventually swings L, keep straight on over a stile and along the side of a field to the A423. Cross with care!

Go over a field and through a beautiful patch of woodland know locally as Bluebell Wood. Descend gradually and turn R along Fineacre Lane back to Stretton.

The view ahead of All Saint's Church on a hilltop above the village is a glorious sight. Stretton is an interesting mixture of the old and the new and is well-worth exploring.

Brinklow

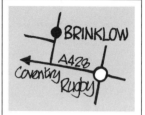

Start/finish Brinklow, on the A4455 Fosse Way six miles northwest of Rugby town centre
Parking With consideration on the village main street
Terrain Field paths, lanes, bridleways and quiet minor roads. Some short climbs. Muddy patches after rain
Time Allow three hours
Facilities Two pubs and shops at Brinklow. Pub at Stretton under Fosse
Public Transport Bus route 585 from Rugby town centre
Maps Explorer sheet 222

A bright and breezy walk across open countryside with some good views. It's also a tour of transport links old and new – the ancient Fosse Way, the railway, the Oxford Canal and the modern motorway.

1 Go down an alleyway off Main Street and pass a recreation ground. At the bottom of the lane go L over a stile and cross a field to another stile just L of a clump of trees. Turn sharp R and follow the hedge on your R through four fields. Join a bridleway and turn R to cross the delightful little 'Lover's Bridge'.

2 Turn L along Smeaton Lane for a short distance, then go R up a minor road to cross a bridge over the canal and another over the railway. Where the lane swings R, go through a gate straight ahead and up a hill through a small field. Join a track to the M6

motorway. Just before a roadbridge turn R onto a enclosed path alongside the motorway. Descend to a footbridge into a field.

Climb diagonally across a hillside heading for a ruined red-brick building. Bear L onto a bridleway which crosses open farmland to the B4455 Fosse Way. Cross the road onto a path along the edge of a field towards Stretton. Go over a stile and bear L across a field into the village.

'Lover's Bridge' near Brinklow

3 Turn L for a short way along the main street, then turn R down a lane next to the Union Jack Inn. This leads to Newbold Revel, now a training school for prison officers. It was for a while St Paul's teacher training college and originally a grand mansion, built in 1716.

The college is private, so turn R off the drive at the main gate and follow the brookside path outside the grounds. Go over another drive and bear R away from the college playing field to follow Smite Brook.

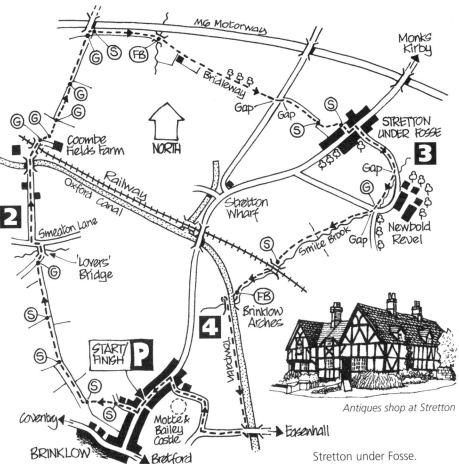

Antiques shop at Stretton

4 Go under the railway to Brinklow Arches, a tunnel in an elevated section of the Oxford canal. Pause to admire the massive structure then go through the tunnel, climb steps on the other side and turn R along the canal towpath. Go under the first bridge you come to and turn R up steps onto the Brinklow to Easenhall road.

Keep on the road to the first junction keeping an eye open for traffic around the corners. Turn R at the first junction onto a minor road and climb a steep hill. Pause at the top to look back over the early part of the walk to the M6 and

Brinklow Arches

Stretton under Fosse.

After appreciating what an excellent viewpoint this hill is, continue along the road to the remains of a Motte and Bailey Castle, built in Norman times to guard the Fosse Way. The road continues into the village down very steep Ell Street (which it probably is if you're labouring up it!)

Turn L along the main street to pass a delightful terrace of cottages and the crumbling 14th century church of St John the Baptist.

The Crown at Stockton

Stockton and Broadwell are both attractive, off the beaten track villages. This walk across open farmland links them and includes a busy section of the Grand Union canal. It also passes four pubs.

Start/finish Broadwell, off the A426 seven miles southwest of Rugby town centre. Or at Stockton, two miles further on
Parking Village hall car parks at Broadwell and Stockton
Terrain Field paths, bridleway, canal towpath and quiet minor roads. Some climbing
Time Allow three hours
Facilities Shops and two pubs at Stockton. Two canal-side pubs
Public Transport Bus route 63 from Clifton Rd, Rugby
Maps Explorer sheet 222

1 From Broadwell green walk through the quiet village to Broadwell House cross-country course. Turn R through two gates and join a bridleway going round the edges of a field. Go L through a gap in a hedge and diagonally across the next field to fence number 13 on the equestrian course. Continue to fence number 15 and turn R to follow the hedge on your R.

Keep straight on across two fields to a minor road and the Grand Union canal. Cross Tomlow Bridge and go through light woodland which covers the disused Leamington to Daventry railway line. When you reach a minor road go R along it for a short while

then turn L down a lane towards Tomlow Farm. At a small plantation before the farm go over a stile on your R and cross a field to a fence stile. Pick your way across three fields to rejoin the minor road on the edge of a disused clay pit.

2 This section is not particularly walker-friendly or interesting. So if you prefer, stay on the minor road, which passes a gallery in one of the disused clay pit buildings.

Stockton locks

A 20 million years-old dinosaur fossil, over 19 feet long, was found during excavation of Blue Lias from the pit in 1898.

Continue into Stockton and turn L into Post Office Lane opposite the village hall. The Barley Mow stands at the end of the lane with St Michael's church – built of locally dug Blue Lias – nearby.

Walk up the rising road away from the church, pass the post office and keep straight on into an enclosed path. The going is quite

34

steep now, so you may wish to take advantage of the fallen tree trunk that a local wag has labelled 'Rest ye awhile seat'. At the top of the hill cross a field to the Dunchurch to Southam road.

3 Cross the road and enter an enclosed pathway. Keep straight on past farm buildings and through light woodland. When you emerge, and with tall factory buildings on your L, turn R through a gap in the hedge, then immediately turn L onto a path along the other side of the hedge. Go through a wood and emerge at Stockton Reservoir, a lovely peaceful spot for wild fowl and fisherfolk.

Bear R through gates to the Blue Lias, a popular canal-side hostelry where temptation to rest awhile should not be resisted. Go on, you deserve it.

Resume walking over the nearby canal bridge and onto the towpath. For the

Broadwell village green

next mile enjoy picturesque canal boats negotiating eight locks. Thirsty work. Fortunately, beyond the top lock there's another canal-side pub, The Boat, where boat people (and walkers) can recover.

4 Go under the canal bridge by The Boat and keep walking until you're level with a short junction amongst trees on the far side of the canal. Here,

turn L through a gap in the hedge, cross the minor road which runs alongside the canal, and go over a stile into a field.

Cross three fields, keeping to the hedge on your L. In the fourth field cross to the far corner but don't go over a stile in front of you. Instead, turn R and follow the hedge on your L up a hill.

Cross the road at the top and go over a field to join the obvious green lane back into the centre of Broadwell where cottages stand prettily around a raised village green.

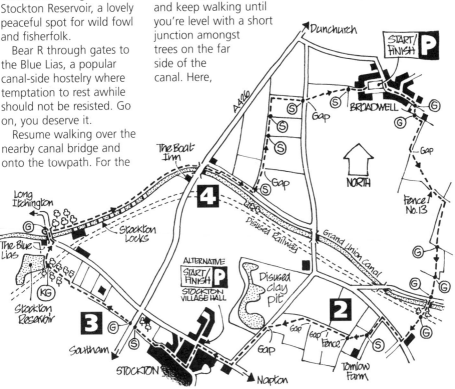

Thurlaston from Toft

The villages of Dunchurch and Thurlaston are always worth visiting – especially on foot. This walk also crosses a manicured golf course, climbs to a good viewpoint and ends with a meander along the shore of Draycote Water.

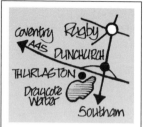

Start & Finish Dunchurch, on the A426. three miles south of Rugby town centre
Parking Dunchurch Square or with consideration on the streets
Terrain Field paths, and quiet minor roads. Some gentle climbing and mud after rain
Time Allow three hours
Facilities Shops and pubs in Dunchurch village
Public Transport Bus routes 563, and 580 from Rugby town centre
Maps Explorer sheet 222

1 Begin walking out of Dunchurch along Southam Road. Cross the bridge over the M45 and, at a post box, turn R down a lane. When a view of Draycote Water appears, turn R over a stile into a field. Go down the hill past a field where, if you're lucky, alpacas run free.

Climb gently across fields to Thurlaston. Swing L onto a lane into the village. Turn R at St Edmund's church, built as the village school in 1847, and follow Church Lane to a junction. Cross the road and turn L along the pavement. Just before the garden with a white dovecote, turn R along

an enclosed pathway. Follow the obvious path down a hill. Go over the stile at the bottom beside an attractive pond and climb another hill, keeping to the hedge on your R, to a road.

Turn L along the road for about 20 yards then turn R at some farm buildings. Do not follow the green lane

Draycote Water ahead

ahead. Instead turn L through a gateway to find a stile into a field. Cross the large field to a stile into Whitefields Golf Course. Look out for stray golf balls and follow the hedge on your R for about 700 yards to the 18th tee.

2 Go down a slope and follow the edge of a pool round L to a stile on your R. Cross the disused Rugby to Leamington railway and continue straight ahead across a rising crop field. Follow the footpath signs along the edge of the next field,

36

then diagonally across another crop field to a minor road.

Turn L down the unfenced road from where there's a fine view, including Draycote Water, ahead. Go under the railway bridge at the bottom of the hill, then turn L into Draycote Fields Nature Reserve.

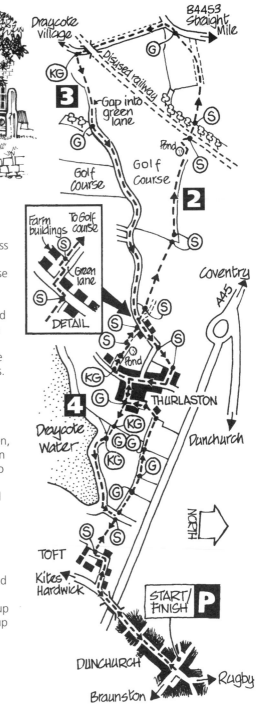

Thurlaston stocks

3 Cross a rising field to a green lane. Keep to the hedge on your L and cross the next open field into a lane. This takes you through another part of the golf course and back into Thurlaston village.

Keep on the road, passing the point where you crossed it earlier. When the road turns sharp R, keep straight on over a stile into an enclosed path. This soon opens to Stocks Lane, which takes you to the village centre and – surprise surprise! – the stocks. Turn R along the road through the village.

Opposite the visitors entrance to Warwickshire Nursing Home, turn L down Church Lane, retracing your earlier route. Where the road swings left at a small green, keep straight on through a gate bearing an instruction to keep to the cement road. Go down the hill and through a couple of kissing gates onto the tarmac road around Draycote Water.

4 Turn L along the road from where there's some good views across the water. Go past a wild fowl reserve, then where the road curves R amongst trees, turn L through a gate onto the private road you crossed earlier.

Turn R to a stile and retrace your steps up the hill (which seems a lot steeper going up than coming down!) to Toft and the lane back onto the main Southam road. Turn L for a gentle stroll back into Dunchurch.

The village is well-worth exploring. For more details see walk 5 on page 12.

37

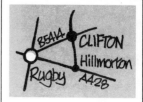

Hillmorton locks

This route straddles the A5, the border between Warwickshire and Northamptonshire. It starts across surprisingly hilly country, levels out through the surreal landscape of tall masts around Rugby Radio Station and ends with a quiet stroll along the canal from the pretty locks and boatyard at Hillmorton.

Start/finish Clifton upon Dunsmore, on Clifton Road, two miles east of Rugby town centre
Parking Recycling Centre car park beside the church
Terrain Field paths, canal towpath, bridleway and quiet minor roads. Some climbing and mud after rain
Time Allow three hours
Facilities Pub and shops at Clifton
Public Transport Bus route 2 from Rugby town centre
Map Explorer sheet 222

1 Start outside Clifton church and walk along the Lilbourne road to the edge of the village. Turn L down Buckwell Lane and go past Manor Farm onto a track. Follow the hedge on your R across three fields. Bear L downhill in the next field and go through twin metal gates and over a footbridge onto the bank of the River Avon.

Follow the hedge on your L which borders Clifton Lakes Farm, a fishery and wild life park established in disused gravel pits. Climb a hill to twin metal gates into a field. Keep to the wire fence on your L around the edge of the field, which over-looks a fishing lake imaginatively constructed from a disused railway cutting on the old Rugby to Market Harborough line.

Go through another set of twin metal gates and straight across the A5 road. TAKE CARE. The A5 is a fast road, but here the visibility is good in both directions so there's no need to take risks.

Go down the road embankment and climb a wooden fence in the hedge into a field. Follow the hedge on your L for a while, then gradually climb across a hillside aiming L of an electric pylon on the skyline. Keep straight on to an arrowhead of hedges on the hilltop, from where there's a great view back across the valley to Catthorpe.

2 Join a track L of a hedge and keep on it over a hill. Descending towards a small wood, turn R through a gap in a scraggy hedge and climb straight up the next field to a stile seen on the skyline. A mound

Catthorpe

on the top of the hill is the remains of a Motte and Bailey castle, a medieval fortification.

Follow the fence around the wood and turn L through a gate. Keep straight on down a hill and through All Saint's churchyard. Mounds across the road from the church are the remains of more Motte and Bailey fortifications.

Turn R along the road from the church. At the first junction, go through a signed kissing gate into a field. Keep to the hedge L and climb to an enclosed pathway. This leads to Lilbourne green, a good place to pause awhile.

3 Resume walking down Hillmorton Lane. When you reach the A5, turn L across the bridge which marks the county border. With care, cross the A5 to a black cinder track opposite. This takes you through an amazing landscape of dozens of huge radio masts apparently sprouting from Warwickshire farmland.

After about a mile of fairly rough walking on a rutted lane you come to Hillmorton Locks. Cross a canal bridge and turn R onto the towpath, a good place to watch the boats.

4 Continue along the towpath to bridge 69. Go onto the bridge and

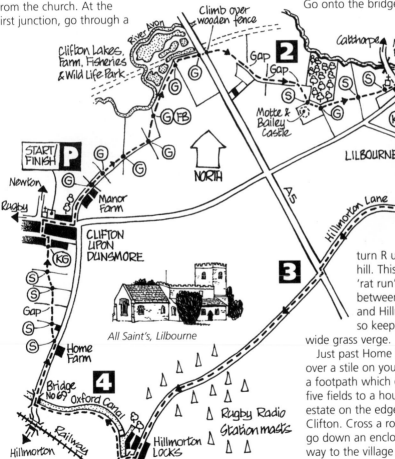

Climb over wooden fence

River Avon

Clifton Lakes, Farm, Fisheries & Wild Life Park

2
Gap
Gap

Catthorpe

Motte & Bailey Castles

KG

Motte & Bailey Castle

KG

LILBOURNE

START/FINISH **P**

Newton

Rugby

Manor Farm

NORTH

A5

Hillmorton Lane

CLIFTON UPON DUNSMORE

All Saint's, Lilbourne

3

KG

S
S
Gap
S
S

Home Farm

Bridge No 69 **4** Oxford Canal

Railway

Hillmorton

Hillmorton Locks

Hillmorton

Rugby Radio Station masts

turn R up a steep hill. This road is a 'rat run' for cars between Clifton and Hillmorton, so keep to the wide grass verge.

Just past Home Farm, go over a stile on your L onto a footpath which crosses five fields to a housing estate on the edge of Clifton. Cross a road and go down an enclosed pathway to the village centre. A stroll round Clifton to round off the walk is highly recommended.

39

Swinford

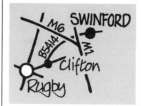

Start/finish Swinford, on minor roads five miles northwest of Rugby town centre
Parking With consideration on the village streets. Stanford Road below the pub is a good bet
Terrain Field paths, bridleway and quiet minor roads. Some gentle climbing
Time Allow 3 hours
Facilities Swinford village pub, Chequers
Public Transport Bus routes 140/141 from Clifton Road, Rugby
Maps Explorer sheets 222 & 223

Based at the pretty village of Swinford, this is a splendid walk across peaceful farmland with some excellent panoramic views across the Leicestershire and Northamptonshire countryside. There are also tempting glimpses of Stamford Hall and its estate.

1 Begin walking along the Kilworth road to the top end of Swinford village. Where the road swings R and with a row of houses ahead on your L, turn R at the brow of the bend to go over a stile into a field where there are some ancient goal posts. Head diagonally over the field, passing the corner of another field on your L.

Cross a stile and continue straight on downhill across the next field to a foot-bridge. Climb a hill in the next field, keeping L of an electricity pylon. Keep walking in a straight line across the next three fields with a wood on your R.

When you reach a track crossing your route, go over a stile and turn R down a hill

to a minor road. Turn R along the road to savour the sight of Stamford Hall along an avenue of trees. It's the only view of the Hall on this route.

2 Cross the bridge over the Avon. Where the road begins to straighten out, turn L onto a bridleway through a wide gap in the hedge. Keep to the obvious route along the edge of a large field.

A memorial at the centre of the field marks the spot

The rear of Stanford Hall

where the pioneer aviator, Percy Pilcher, crashed an experimental glider in 1898, while using Stanford Hall as a base. He was one of the first people to die in an air accident.

Cross the embankment of the disused Rugby to Market Harborough railway line and continue straight across the next field to a minor road to Cold Ashby.

Turn L along the road and climb steadily up a hill to Park Farm. Turn R at the far end of the farm buildings. Go past some silos, then turn R again to find the start of a bridleway going across high ground on your L.

A wonderful mile of walking follows, as you traverse a grassy ridge with splendid views on all sides.

Chequers

3 At Stanford Mear farm, cross the Stanford to Clay Coton road. Have a look at the old boundary stone pillars at the side of the road.

Rejoin the bridleway on the other side of road where it has deteriorated to a faint path across the topside of a sloping field. Keep to the hedge on your L and go through a gate into the next field.

Continue downhill bearing R to an iron gate in the centre of the hedge in front of you.

Cross the next large field, heading for the far corner where a line of trees joins the embankment of the A14 trunk road. The trees actually hide the end another section of the disused railway, which you should cross. Enter a long narrow field and head across the centre, keeping parallel with the A14.

4 When you get close to some large signs on the roadside L, bear R across the field to a series of stiles and a couple of

footbridges over the River Avon. Excellent waymarking now directs you away from the noisy A14 and over three fields to join the road back into the Swinford. A tour of the village and its beautiful church is highly recommended, followed perhaps with refreshment at Chequers, a traditional village pub.

Stanford Hall
William and Mary house on the banks of the River Avon. Open to the public with a motorcycle museum, teashop and special events. There's also on show a full size replica of the 1898 Percy Pilcher flying machine

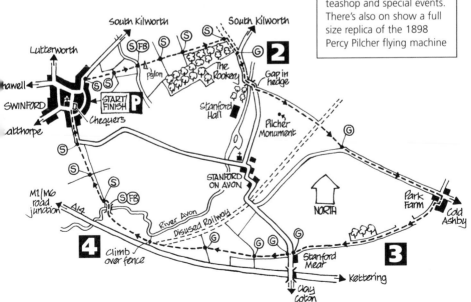

Ashby St Ledgers

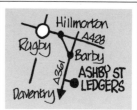

Start/finish Ashby St Ledgers, off the A361 Kilsby to Daventry road seven miles southeast of Rugby town centre
Parking With consideration on the village main street
Terrain Field paths, lanes, bridleway and quiet minor roads. Some gentle climbing and mud after rain
Time Allow 3 hours
Facilities Pub in Ashby St Ledgers. Two pubs and shops in Braunston
Public Transport None
Map Explorer sheet 222

A wonderful walk across open, rolling countryside, full of variety and with fine views. The route links two of the most attractive villages in the area. Each has its own distinct character yet is totally different from the other. Compare, contrast and enjoy.

1 From Ashby St Ledgers cross straight over the Kilsby to Daventry road (with care!) to join a signed bridleway climbing the hill in front of you. This is part of the Jurassic Way, named after the belt of Jurassic limestone it runs along.

Descend slightly to the Barby to Welton minor road. Turn R along it for approx 50 yards then turn L onto the signed route to Braunston. There's extensive views across the village to Napton and round to Draycote Water on the R. Continue downhill and join a lane into Braunston.

2 Keep straight on along the long main street. Pass the village green, The Wheatsheaf and The Plough (circa 1672) public houses and

many attractive houses of mellow Northamptonshire stone.

At the end of the street turn R around magnificent All Saints Church and continue along the road into a modern housing estate. Keep on the road to a footpath sign (opposite the Plough car park).

Turn L down an enclosed pathway between houses. Keep straight on through a close to a road. Turn R

Braunston

along it for a short distance then turn L down 'Countryside' which curves L down a hill. You will soon see a gap between the houses straight ahead.

Go over a stile and straight across a paddock. Cross another stile and climb a long, narrow field. The Oxford canal is seen across to your L and there's a terrific view back across the village.

3 Keep straight on through a series of waymarked fields. At Braunston Fields farm, bear L aiming for Willoughby Fields on the hillside ahead. Find a stile

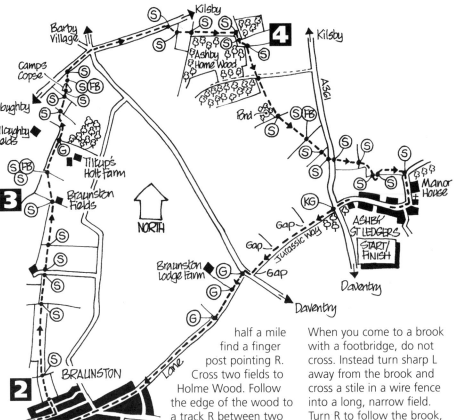

and footbridge combination through a tall hedge and follow the course of the wooded stream on your L up a cleft in the hills.

At a gate below Tiltup's Wood, keep straight on up the hillside and cross two fields to Camps Copse, a patch of fruit trees with a seat to admire the view.

Continue to climb, then turn R along the Willoughby road. At a crossroads by a watertower and radio mast keep straight on to join the road signed 'Kilsby'. After about half a mile find a finger post pointing R. Cross two fields to Holme Wood. Follow the edge of the wood to a track R between two patches of woodland.

4 At the end of the track bear L to cross a stile and climb the gently rising hill with the wood R. This is a beautiful area of estate-managed woodland and rolling fields. Don't be surprised to come across pheasants and wildfowl. At the top of the hill cross a track and continue in an almost straight line across four well-signed fields to the Kilsby to Daventry road.

Cross with care and continue straight across a gently descending field with Asby St Ledgers R.

When you come to a brook with a footbridge, do not cross. Instead turn sharp L away from the brook and cross a stile in a wire fence into a long, narrow field. Turn R to follow the brook, then bear L through a patch of Scots Pine trees to a stile into a lane.

Turn R to pass the ancient Manor House, where the Gunpowder Plot was allegedly hatched, the weathered 14th century church of St Leodegarius (Ledger) and the rest of this remarkably peaceful and picturesque village.

Part of the Manor House

43